SLEEPING BEAUTY...

This devotional was birthed out of frustrations, conversations, prayer, and time with God. I am not perfect but I am a daughter of the King. Therefore, I have rights and it was time to understand the privileges associated with that. I wanted to know more about my identity in Christ so I started to ask questions. That is the format for how I outlined this book which is more like a conversation.

So why call it Sleeping Beauty? I felt like I was watching my life happen to me, sleepwalking through the entire thing. Missing out on opportunities, understanding and the inability to live in the moment. I was this beautiful masterpiece that everyone could see but me. How would I become an active participant in His will for my life? It wasn't until I discovered who I was in Christ that I could appreciate how He created me. It's something about seeing yourself the way the creator sees you that speaks to your being. I heard Him say that it was time to get up and walk in my purpose. Through this He took me on a journey of healing and revelation. It is my prayer that this devotional will help set you free to arise and walk in the full power and authority of Christ who lives in you. The truth is, it isn't always easy to come out of the sunken place. I went through a series of setbacks that made me feel like it wasn't going to happen or that I was forgotten. However, the Lord was waking me up from the realities of life and into the truth of who I am. The redeemer is here and despite what you have been through, you will recover all. Welcome to your refresh, it's not over yet. And with that I am extending an invitation to you, inviting Christ into this moment of your life for a renewed sense of power, strength and identity.

Father, I thank you for your daughter reading this right now, I thank you for the new thing you are doing in her heart. I ask that you release and reveal all distractions preventing her from getting closer to you. I pray that the scales would fall from her eyes unveiling her beauty and value. I praise you for the revelation and strategy that you are downloading. I pray that she finds herself submerged in a love affair with you. I invite you into every aspect of her life, revealing secrets and tearing down strongholds. She belongs to you Father and as a result her freedom is a birthright. I pray that she will find her authority and voice in you. We violently take back everything that was lost, stolen, abandoned and deprived from her. Be the balm in Gilead that releases healing, clarity and affirms her place in you. I declare peace and victory over her, she will hear from you, her mind and body are healed and every part of her will come into proper alignment with the word of Christ that was spoken over her. I thank you for life, for second chances and an opportunity to do it again. For the second wind you have provided, for your grace, for your mercy and most importantly for your love. I ask you for forgiveness for putting fear in place of purpose and identity. Help your daughter to be the daughter You have called her to be. Amen.

As you read this devotional, write and record the revelation that the Lord gives you. Also, make a list of the things you are believing God for.

Contents

Sleeping Beauty...

Woman of God Arise

BRITTANY R. STEWART

Brittany Stewart

Day 1-Are You Willing To Give It Up?

Mathew 27:46-53 AMP

45 Now from the sixth hour (noon) there was darkness over all the land until the ninth hour (3:00 p.m.). 46 About the ninth hour Jesus cried out with a loud [agonized] voice, "Eli, Eli, lama sabachthani?" that is, "My God, My God, why have You forsaken Me?" 47 When some of the bystanders there heard it, they began saying, "This man is calling for Elijah." 48 Immediately one of them ran, and took a sponge, soaked it with sour wine and put it on a reed, and gave Him a drink. 49 But the rest said, "Let us see whether Elijah will come to save Him [from death]." 50 And Jesus cried out again with a loud [agonized] voice, and gave up His spirit [voluntarily, sovereignly dismissing and releasing His spirit from His body in submission to His Father's plan]. 51 And [at once] the veil [of the Holy of Holies] of the temple was torn in two from top to bottom; the earth shook and the rocks were split apart. 52 The tombs were opened, and many bodies of the saints (God's people) who had fallen asleep [in death] were raised [to life]; 53 and coming out of the tombs after His resurrection, they entered the holy city (Jerusalem) and appeared to many people.

It's generally in your darkest place that God can provide the most light, but it's getting to the light that we struggle with. The process of getting out of dark situations or reaching the next level often involves a commitment to giving something up. A surrender. We generally reach this place once we get past the frustration of our emotions. The Bible says (Mathew 27:46) he cried " My God, My God why have you forsaken Me?" God had to get him to a place where there were no distractions on a level where nothing could take him from his purpose. I know you're thinking well why couldn't He have just gone to the mountains to get away like He did before? Because He was at a new level. He was at a point where the Lord wasn't going to allow Him to turn back. On the mountainside He was still accessible. People could still reach Him if they needed to, but here on this cross it was just Him and God. He had no choice but to release His spirit and give everything up. (Mathew 27:50) God is calling for us to release our own spirit, our flesh, our desires and our will so that He can take us to the next level and remove us out of dark situations. Once this happens the real purpose or work is able to go forth. Prophecy could not have been fulfilled without Him releasing his spirit. The best part about this scripture is not only the veil being ripped breaking down our communication walls with God (giving us liberty to talk to the Lord directly), but the tombs opening and the saints (I love the way the Amp version puts this) who had fallen asleep were raised to life. It's something about God bringing you out of that dark place and giving you life. Meaning that slump you've been in, that depression that's tried to overtake you has no power when the commitment is made, when we release our own spirit to God. He is then allowed to bring forth life in us. This is what Jesus died for, this is why we can rejoice in the Lord with Him being our strength because although our situations have made us feel dead, dead to our emotions, to our reality. He comes in like the loving Father that He is and brings us new life.

Prayer:

Father I thank you, that Your name is great, I thank you that there is a plan and a purpose over my life. I am honored to be chosen by you. I ask that you help me to release all things that would distract me or deter me from my purpose in You. I ask for understanding on how to surrender myself fully so that You can have your way in my life. I thank you for taking me out of dark places and bringing me back to life. I commit my life to you. In Jesus name Amen.

Although life circumstances have caused you to fall asleep in your own life, commit to His will, and allow Him to bring you back. What do you need to give up in order for the prophecy to be fulfilled concerning your life? What scares you the most about dying to self?

Day 2-What's Your Safe Place?

Psalms 91 NIV

1 Whoever dwells in the shelter of the Most High will rest in the shadow of the Almighty. 2 I will say of the LORD, "He is my refuge and my fortress, my God, in whom I trust." 3 Surely he will save you from the fowler's snare and from the deadly pestilence. 4 He will cover you with his feathers, and under his wings you will find refuge; his faithfulness will be your shield and rampart. 5 You will not fear the terror of night, nor the arrow that flies by day, 6 nor the pestilence that stalks in the darkness, nor the plague that destroys at midday. 7 A thousand may fall at your side, ten thousand at your right hand, but it will not come near you. 8 You will only observe with your eyes and see the punishment of the wicked. 9 If you say, "The LORD is my refuge," and you make the Most High your dwelling, 10 no harm will overtake you, no disaster will come near your tent. 11 For he will command his angels concerning you to guard you in all your ways; 12 they will lift you up in their hands, so that you will not strike your foot against a stone. 13 You will tread on the lion and the cobra; you will trample the great lion and the serpent. 14 "Because he loves me," says the LORD, "I will rescue him; I will protect him, for he acknowledges my name. 15 He will call on me, and I will answer him; I will be with him in trouble, I will deliver him and honor him. 16 With long life I will satisfy him and show him my salvation."

Life can become overwhelming and consuming with checklists, agendas, deadlines or just trying to figure things out. Especially in transitional seasons, it is easy to want to hide. At least until you can figure it out and grab a hold of what's going on. The best place to hide is in Him. That's the one place no matter who/what is looking for you that you are safe and securely tucked away. Things are not allowed to get to you when you are hiding in Him. This doesn't mean they won't come try to find you, it just means they won't find you. This includes your mind. Taking time to dwell in him allows you to communicate with Him and for Him to communicate with you. It gives you peace over situations and allows God to filter the things that you see and feel so you can see them for what they are and not be confused. Allow God to be your shield. The thing about a shield is that if you don't use it properly it serves no purpose. It's God's desire to protect you, He wants to make sure nothing comes your way to destroy you. He is the ultimate lover. The advantage of being a child of the Most High is that it comes with benefits, all He wants is your Yes, to be your True love. The bible says," I will rescue him, be with him in trouble, deliver and honor him". He just wants to take care of you. This is one of my favorite scriptures because it is written like a love letter. God's just writing to you to remind you that He's in love with you and He will always be your safe place.

Prayer:
Father I thank you that you always have my best interest at heart, that you are the lover of my soul and my place of refuge. I acknowledge you as the love of my life, consistently protecting

and providing for me. Continue to hide me and show me how to rely on you as my secret place. Protecting my mind and my body from the enemy. Be with me always Father, and I will forever give you the glory and praise you deserve. Amen.

Whatever you need Him to be He will be. Cast all your cares on Him. Take shelter in God. Find out what prevents you from taking shelter in God and ignore it. Where is your secret place? What do you hear the Lord saying to you when you are there?

Day 3-Why should I seek Him early?

Proverbs 8:17 AMPC

7 I love those who love me, and those who seek me early and diligently shall find me.

Early in my relationship with God I struggled with really seeking the Lord early, this is in part because I would generally oversleep or wake up tired and running behind. And when I'm running late I would either say a quick little Lord cover me for the day prayer or just skip it and wait until I got home (which was usually late at night). The problem with this was that I was creating a habit of giving everything else (job, friends, etc.) the best parts of me and then whatever was left to God. Thus not involving God in my day or situation "early". It's hard for Him to guide your day or for the Holy Spirt to speak to you about something if you've already started to do without them. It's like asking someone their opinion about something you want to do after you have done it. We tend to totally ignore God or give him our left over energy and then question where was He, when situations arise. God doesn't want to be an after thought. How can he warn you of things to come or present you with opportunities of blessing and favor if you don't talk to Him? What I've learned is God always has an opinion and something to say. Allow Him to create the structure for your day and truly lead you. Another benefit to seeking God early in the morning is at this time you are less likely to encounter distractions. When everyone else is still asleep it provides a space for you to quietly commune with God. This gives Him your full attention. If you really love Him, show Him. Things you love you prioritize and give attention to.

Prayer:

Father, I bless you for being a patient God, for seeking me out early even when I'm not looking for you. I ask that you help me to spend time with you before I do or give energy to anything else. I want you to guide my day through guiding my heart. Download your plans for me and the route you would have me take to get there, become my personal GPS. I move everything to the side and give you all of me first. Help me to be more consistent with allowing you to lead. In Jesus name Amen.

The best way to create an atmosphere for his prescience is to create a space for Him to dwell. Start your day with an atmosphere surrounded by God. What do you need to do to create an atmosphere for him to dwell?

Day 4-Do You Feel Stuck?

Genesis 15:1-4 AMPC

1 After these things, the word of the Lord came to Abram in a vision, saying, Fear not, Abram, I am your Shield, your abundant compensation, and your reward shall be exceedingly great. 2 And Abram said, Lord God, what can You give me, since I am going on [from this world] childless and he who shall be the owner and heir of my house is this [steward] Eliezer of Damascus? 3 And Abram continued, Look, You have given me no child; and [a servant] born in my house is my heir. 4 And behold, the word of the Lord came to him, saying, This man shall not be your heir, but he who shall come from your own body shall be your heir. Now Sarai, Abram's wife, had borne him no children. She had an Egyptian maid whose name was Hagar.

Genesis 16: 2-5 AMPC

2 And Sarai said to Abram, See here, the Lord has restrained me from bearing [children]. I am asking you to have intercourse with my maid; it may be that I can obtain children by her. And Abram listened to and heeded what Sarai said.3 So Sarai, Abram's wife, took Hagar her Egyptian maid, after Abram had dwelt ten years in the land of Canaan, and gave her to her husband Abram to be his [secondary] wife.4 And he had inter-course with Hagar, and she became pregnant; and when she saw that she was with child, she looked with contempt upon her mistress and despised her.5 Then Sarai said to Abram, May [the responsibility for] my wrong and deprivation of rights be upon you! I gave my maid into your bosom, and when she saw that she was with child, I was contemptible and despised in her eyes. May the Lord be the judge between you and me.

In order to write this, I had to use two different scriptures because often as Christians we start off in one place and end in another. That's where we get stuck. Initially we are all excited to follow the will and the word of the Lord (he chose me, he has anointed me type of stuff) which is all great but the challenge comes when we are charged to walk in it. The patience it takes to get to that place, the sacrifice it takes to receive the next set of instructions or even promotion for the next space. We get lost in what we have been called to be and the reality of where we are actually at. So God will give/reveal a promise. And we are excited for the moment, then when it takes longer than we expected we start to take things into our own hands. The Lord had already revealed to Abram that he would give him a child. Why do we think that God needs our help to make things happen? Imagine God in all his sovereignty needing the help of us. The result of us forcing things can bring about other things, unwanted things. God was not finished processing Abram yet, he had not yet changed his name so there were still things that God wanted to show him before this child came. Would Abram have been able to make the same decision Abraham did and follow the instructions of God and sacrifice his son? What about his son Ishmel and the sacrifice of having to send him away, this wouldn't haven't even been an issue if they had just decided to wait. Genesis 15 starts off with the Lord telling him not to fear that He would be his shield, his compensation and that his reward would be great. However, in fear that it wouldn't happen his wife forced a marriage with someone else and produced a baby. He knew the promise, he just didn't believe it.

Prayer:

Father I thank you that the promises of the Lord are yes and Amen. I repent for trying to produce a promise out of my will and not trusting yours. I ask that you help me to be patient and wait on you. Help guard the desires of my heart so that they don't overwhelm me into destruction. I praise your name that you are faithful and you are watching over your word to see it performed. Amen.

Waiting isn't always easy but I've learned that the process is always necessary. God wants to make sure you don't forfeit your promise with a counterfeit. You must believe that it will happen, when it is supposed to happen. What do you kinda believe about your promise?Why do we make the wrong decisions when we clearly know better? What have you settled for (this could be anything in your life that is less than the promise of God)?

Day 5-It's Common Sense Right?

Proverbs 3:21-26 NLT

21 My child, don't lose sight of common sense and discernment. Hang on to them. 22 For they will refresh your soul. They are like jewels on a necklace. 23 They keep you safe on your way, and your feet will not stumble. 24 You can go to bed without fear; you will lie down and sleep soundly. 25 You need not be afraid of sudden disaster or the destruction that comes upon the wicked. 26 for the Lord is your security. He will keep your foot from being caught in a trap.

I love how this verse starts off saying "my child, don't lose sight of common sense and discernment". We easily get caught up in the routine of things and miss the basics of our foundation. Honestly, there are times when I am under high pressure situations and I forget to breathe. There have also been times where I have been so caught up in things, projects and relationships that common sense wasn't so common. Often, God wants us to remember the basics. What do you know to be true ? Does it align with the will and the word for your life? Rely on him and allow him to refresh your soul and keep you out of harm's way. He left us with the Holy Spirit to help guide us. The Holy Spirit operates through discernment letting us know what we should step into and what we should walk away from. It serves as a sign for traps and dangers that could arise. Rest in the safety of God, you got security.

Prayer:
Father, help me to not lose sight of common sense and discernment. Tailor my heart and my mind to yield to your will and promises. I give you permission to be Lord over my emotions, my fears and all anxiety I may be feeling. You are my protection and my light and I trust in you. Amen.

Don't lose sight of common sense and discernment, hang on to them. Have you prayed that God sharpen your discernment? What has the Holy Spirit shown you, tried to prevent you from that you have ignored? What are some of the basics in your relationship with Christ that you need to get back to?

Day 6-You Ready?

Joshua 1:1-9 NLV

1After the death of Moses the Lord's servant, the Lord spoke to Joshua son of Nun, Moses' assistant. He said, 2 "Moses my servant is dead. Therefore, the time has come for you to lead these people, the Israelites, across the Jordan River into the land I am giving them. 3 I promise you what I promised Moses: 'Wherever you set foot, you will be on land I have given you— 4 from the Negev wilderness in the south to the Lebanon mountains in the north, from the Euphrates River in the east to the Mediterranean Sea[a] in the west, including all the land of the Hittites.' 5 No one will be able to stand against you as long as you live. For I will be with you as I was with Moses. I will not fail you or abandon you. 6 "Be strong and courageous, for you are the one who will lead these people to possess all the land I swore to their ancestors I would give them. 7 Be strong and very courageous. Be careful to obey all the instructions Moses gave you. Do not deviate from them, turning either to the right or to the left. Then you will be successful in everything you do. 8 Study this Book of Instruction continually. Meditate on it day and night so you will be sure to obey everything written in it. Only then will you prosper and succeed in all you do. 9 This is my command—be strong and courageous! Do not be afraid or discouraged. For the Lord your God is with you wherever you go."

One of the hardest things in life is to step out from under the shadows of a great leader, the legacy of your family, or what you've been previously known as and move into your new season of independence, opportunity and leadership. It can be scary but know that this is your time to lead, this is your time to move. Joshua's obedience at this point in his life was crucial. It was time sensitive and it carried the weight of the lives of others. With new responsibilities and a new mantle he watched the ways of how the ones who came before him did it and now it was time for him to take the new generation into the promise land. This shift required him to move immediately. If you continue reading you will see that Joshua moved without delay. He had been trained for this moment, prepped and prepared. He moved from the position of the assistant to the boss, and because of his obedience the Israelites would see victories that they had not seen before. He was able to move in boldness because he heard clear instructions from God and He was with him. Joshua had always been a warrior, now he was to operate as the commander.

Prayer:

Father, I thank you for pushing me out of my comfort zone. I thank you that you trust me and with you nothing is impossible. Help me to actively listen to the instructions that you have given so that I may know how to effectively lead. You are the God of all and I yield to the promises you have over my life. Father, I ask that you help me to be obedient and remember that when I am weak that's when you are made strong. You are Emmanuel and through you I am victorious. Amen.

You have been anointed to be great. Remember, "the plans of the Lord stand firm forever". You are prepared and this is your moment! What new roles of leadership or authority have you been given? What is preventing you from moving forward in them? What strategy has the Lord given you to accomplish that?

Day 7-What Do You Hold The Keys To?

Esther 4:13-17 NLV

13 Mordecai sent this reply to Esther: "Don't think for a moment that because you're in the palace you will escape when all other Jews are killed. 14 If you keep quiet at a time like this, deliverance and relief for the Jews will arise from some other place, but you and your relatives will die. Who knows if perhaps you were made queen for just such a time as this?" 15 Then Esther sent this reply to Mordecai: 16 "Go and gather together all the Jews of Susa and fast for me. Do not eat or drink for three days, night or day. My maids and I will do the same. And then, though it is against the law, I will go in to see the king. If I must die, I must die." 17 So Mordecai went away and did everything as Esther had ordered him.

Women have been given a great power of influence. Influence to shift nations, kingships and even the hearts of men. Esther had the favor of the king and because of this she had to use it to help bring deliverance to her people. While reading the story of Esther, I often think of that deep sigh of relief she must have had finally making it into the palace (her place of wealth, status, influence etc.) That she finally had a moment to just relax and take it all in. She had been delivered out of her past season so this must be her season to rest. However, this wasn't just about her own deliverance (coming into oneself) but it was about the deliverance of a people. The grace on her life was tied to the ones who came before her and the ones who would come after. She risked it all to change the future of her people. This actually ties to the great commission- Matthew 28:20 " and teaching them to obey everything I have commanded you. And surely I am with you always, to the very end of the age." We are all seeds of influence, some of us will plant, some of us will water and some of us will pull the harvest out of the ground. This may be your season to unlock the door for someone else.

Prayer:

Father, I thank you for the way that you have created me. I ask you to forgive me for not always using my influence to bring light to other people. I am honored that you would choose and create me this way and I do not take it lightly. Help me to move fearlessly into the person of influence you have called me to be. Help me to teach and obey everything that you have commanded of me. I have been created for such a time as this use me and my influence for your glory. Amen.

Influence brings forth responsibility and" to whom much is given, much is required". What do you have influence over? Who are the individuals attached to your deliverance? Are you willing to risk it all to help set your people free? What is your job/responsibility right now?

Day 8-Have You Gotten To Know Grace?

Hebrews 4:14-16 NIV

14 Therefore, since we have a great high priest who has ascended into heaven, Jesus the Son of God, let us hold firmly to the faith we profess. 15 For we do not have a high priest who is unable to empathize with our weaknesses, but we have one who has been tempted in every way, just as we are—yet he did not sin. 16 Let us then approach God's throne of grace with confidence, so that we may receive mercy and find grace to help us in our time of need.

Read that scripture again but this time say it with some authority. Grace has honestly been one of the hardest things for me to understand. For many years religion represented rules and an idea of perfection that was rewarded with grace from God. It was the idea that if I do this, then I will get that. I believe many doors closed because I closed them not believing that I deserved for them to be open. Thinking like that was a problem because I was treating God like a gum ball machine. With the belief that as long as I pay the right price, I will get the prize. However, if I mess up my prayers deserve to not get answered. I would try to be perfect or do things in my own strength just to prove that I'm worth it. Through my own oversight, I missed the grace of God, the Father, the one who loves unconditionally, who would keep and protect me no matter what. I would constantly equate my shortcomings and those of others as a reset, that must be dealt with through punishment. Like a child waiting to be reprimanded I would justify the negative part of my story, that I deserve it because of sin. Continuously finding myself stuck (paralyzed), and unable to move into my next. Forfeiting the promise of God, the one who desires for me to live blessed. I am so thankful we have a Father that continues to remind us we are worth it, simply because He is our Father. Not because we deserve it or are perfect but because He is. Christ is not some Santa, there is no list he's checking twice or comparing my shortcomings to. He loves me because I am His. He encourages us daily to come to his throne of grace, receive his grace and allow his grace to help us. This is because solutions are found in him. Rest, peace and power are found in him. We can relax because He got this and He got us.

Prayer:

Father help me to see myself the way that you see me. Help me to understand your grace and favor toward me and that the price was paid for me years ago on the cross. You are not like man, help me to understand the love of the Father and the breakthrough that if affords me. I don't have to be perfect because You are. Amen.

I think it is important to look up the definition of grace and see if you can find examples in your life that support how He has demonstrated that grace to you. Let this be a reminder that no matter what you are going through, there is grace for that. Where have you found grace with God? What has been your relationship with grace? What has grace afforded you?

Day 9-How Will You Protect Your Sacrifice?

Genesis 15:8-11 NLT

8 But Abram replied, "O Sovereign Lord, how can I be sure that I will actually possess it?" 9 The Lord told him, "Bring me a three-year-old heifer, a three-year-old female goat, a three-year-old ram, a turtledove, and a young pigeon." 10 So Abram presented all these to him and killed them. Then he cut each animal down the middle and laid the halves side by side; he did not, however, cut the birds in half.11 Some vultures swooped down to eat the carcasses, but Abram chased them away.

Someone once told me that I never finish anything. Like all the time I had set aside was for nothing. This was hard for me to hear because I knew some aspects of it to be true. This was said to me in the midst of writing this journal. And, for the most part I had the majority of it complete but just never got around to making the edits and publishing it. However, before I knew it an entire year had passed by and there was no finished product to show. I had sacrificed, had scriptures on sticky notes but allowed the vultures to swoop down and eat the remains of the directions the Lord gave me. I allowed people and the busyness of absolutely nothing to take away the sacrifice I had just made. I am telling you from experience, you have to protect the sacrifice you (the things you have surrendered)made unto the Lord. A Lot of us do the work to get in front of the Lord, then allow distractions to come and descend upon our ideas, our quiet time with him or even the things we are supposed to produce. You have to learn to guard your sacrifice.

Prayer:
Father, help me protect the things I've laid on the altar to you. Help me to not come off of my post but to guard it day and night. I declare a divorce between myself and distractions. I will possess what the Lord has for me and I will let nothing come between me and my promise. In Jesus name, Amen.

The road to accomplish anything does not come without sacrifice and that sacrifice doesn't produce anything without you protecting it. I think it is important to explore the definition of sacrifice in order to put the word in context. According to the Oxford American Dictionary, a sacrifice is "...surrendering a possession as an offering to God.." and/or " an act of giving up something values for the sake of something else regarded as more important or worthy". I dare you to take authority over your promise, your directions, your sacrifice and chase away anything that comes against the will of your life. What have you sacrificed in order to accomplish something? What has descended upon it to distract you or take you away from it? How will you chase it away?

Day 10-What Is Hiding Among You?

Joshua 7:13 NLT

13"Get up! Command the people to purify themselves in preparation for tomorrow. For this is what the Lord, the God of Israel, says: Hidden among you, O Israel, are things set apart for the Lord. You will never defeat your enemies until you remove these things from among you.

The lord will get you to a place where he starts to point out things that may-be prolonging the process. This generally comes through sanctification. Getting to a space where you have purified (holiness) yourself in preparation for what to-morrow will bring. Then He starts to show you what needs to be removed in order for you to get to your next. This process is called deliverance. Reaching new levels in Christ requires the removal of some of the things we held so precious and dear. During this process we are forced to confront and make a decision about what will continue with us on our journey. I love analyzing the tone of this text, " Get up ! Command the people..." The Lord is giving you a command and he is challenging you to get things in order. You are currently in preparation for tomorrow, the Lord has already promised you victory. The defeat of your enemies belongs to you if only you would remove the things hidden. The word hidden sticks out because that means that these things will not be in plain sight. Some of these things will only be revealed through the separation that takes place through sanctification.

Prayer:

Father, show me what holiness is. I give you permission to show me what is hidden among me that I need to let go of so that I may move forward. My deliverance starts today, no more defeat because I have the tools to overcome that which has tried to overtake me. Help me to use the authority I have been given to command the things in my life to get in order in accordance to your will. Amen.

There are big things that the Lord is trying to prepare you for, enemies you are destined to defeat and take down. Joshua was leading men and setting the groundwork for his victory as well as the victory of others. What does sanctification/purity look like for your everyday life? What things are hidden among you that are prolonging your process?

Day 11-How Attached Are You To Your Trauma?

Exodus 14:10-14 NIV

10 As Pharaoh approached, the Israelites looked up, and there were the Egyptians, marching after them. They were terrified and cried out to the Lord. 11 They said to Moses, "Was it because there were no graves in Egypt that you brought us to the desert to die? What have you done to us by bringing us out of Egypt? 12 Didn't we say to you in Egypt, 'Leave us alone; let us serve the Egyptians'? It would have been better for us to serve the Egyptians than to die in the desert!" 13 Moses answered the people, "Do not be afraid. Stand firm and you will see the deliverance the Lord will bring you today. The Egyptians you see today you will never see again. 14 The Lord will fight for you; you need only to be still."

On the journey to my promise you have no idea how many times I have asked to be taken back to the wilderness, back to an ex, back to what was comfortable or simply just back to the last place I felt safe. Stepping out on faith and making a decision to live for Christ isn't always easy. It requires you to walk it out, die to old mindsets and old versions of yourself.

I have definitely panicked when I saw the " Egyptians" (past relationships, promises broken, abuse etc.) that I thought were defeated rear their ugly heads. But I've had to learn to put the word up against how I am feeling. "Don't be afraid. Just stand still and watch the Lord Rescue you today". These enemies are not reality and you will not be ruled by your emotions. The enemy knows that there is a promise for you, just as there was a promise for the people of Israel. You have nothing to be afraid of " The Lord himself will fight for you, you need just hold your peace" You are no longer a slave, you do not have a slave mindset and it is the will of the Lord for you to walk in freedom and prosper. I know how easy it is to rehearse what life was like before, what you thought you had and how comfortable you may have felt but I challenge you to stand still and hold your peace.

Prayer:

Father, I thank you that you fight on my behalf. I thank you that the promises of the Lord are yes and Amen. Teach me how to put all of my trust in you. Teach me how to trust you and move forward. I ask that you guard my eyes and my ears so that they decipher truth vs. reality. Help me to divorce my relationship with dysfunction and live in your promise. I thank you for your protection. Amen.

The Israelites were so scared and shook with fear that they did not want to move on. They preferred being a slave, because they knew what to expect as a slave. Stepping out and walking into promise will push you past your comfort zone, but I invite you to keep walking and moving forward. Watch the Lord deliver you today, stay calm He got this. How do you relate to the Israelites? Have you identified your Egyptians?

Day 12-Have You Made It Obey?

2 Corinthians 10:3-5 NIV

3 For though we live in the world, we do not wage war as the world does. 4 The weapons we fight with are not the weapons of the world. On the contrary, they have divine power to demolish strongholds. 5 We demolish arguments and every pretension that sets itself up against the knowledge of God, and we take captive every thought to make it obedient to Christ.

This has to be one of my favorite scriptures. I literally repeat verse 5 " Take captive every thought that would exalt itself above the knowledge of Christ" over and over to help put my mind into perspective. It serves as a reminder and notice to all the things that would come up against the knowledge (the truth) of Christ and make it obey (submit) to the promise of God concerning you. The evil one likes to attack in the area of your mind playing with the thought that the promises that the Lord has spoken over your life are empty. However, that is so far from the truth. Being able to take captive the thoughts and force it to submit to the knowledge(power and authority) of Christ is a real strategy. The bible then goes on to say make it obey.

Prayer:

Father help me to walk in the full power and authority you have given me. Teach me what my weapons are and give me strategies on how to use them. Guard my mind against the thoughts and ideas that are not of you. I speak death to every word curse and or negative thought that has been spoken. Even the negative thoughts and words I have said about myself must submit to the word and knowledge of Christ, I repent for believing the lies of the enemy. Negativity you must go now, you no longer have access to me. I declare the favor and blessing of the Lord over me. I declare proverbs 10:22 over me " The blessings of the Lord maketh rich and addeth no sorrow". Amen.

So make your situation obedient to Him, that's the real power and that the real authority you have. You have the authority to take back the things that belong to you, that includes your identity, your mind and your peace. Are you demolishing strongholds or coming into agreement with them?

Day 13-Who Do You Need To Put Out?

Mark 5: 35-43 NIV

35 While Jesus was still speaking, some people came from the house of Jairus, the synagogue leader. "Your daughter is dead," they said. "Why bother the teacher anymore?" 36 Overhearing they said, Jesus told him, "Don't be afraid; just believe." 37 He did not let anyone follow him except Peter, James and John the brother of James. 38 When they came to the home of the synagogue leader, Jesus saw a commotion, with people crying and wailing loudly. 39 He went in and said to them, "Why all this commotion and wailing? The child is not dead but asleep." 40 But they laughed at him. After he put them all out, he took the child's father and mother and the disciples who were with him, and went in where the child was. 41 He took her by the hand and said to her, "Talitha koum!" (which means "Little girl, I say to you, get up!"). 42 Immediately the girl stood up and began to walk around (she was twelve years old). At this they were completely astonished. 43 He gave strict orders not to let anyone know about this, and told them to give her something to eat.

Sometimes inviting others on the journey with you can be a hindrance. One of the most heartbreaking parts of my journey was realizing that everyone couldn't come with me. I imagine that had to be hard for the family members in the house when Jesus came to heal that little girl. Who is he to clear them out of the house? They had known her longer, he couldn't have possibly cared about her more than they did. When the Lord is dealing(healing or working) with you he will clear the room, and often everyone can't be a part of that process. Some will say they believe and don't really believe. While others will want to watch just to see if you fail. The Father used this as an opportunity to silence the naysayers and create an atmosphere for healing and breakthrough to go forth. People had already started to declare death over the situation but the Lord was not finished yet.

Prayer:
Father I bless your name, I thank you for your love and kindness. I thank you for the promise you have given me. I thank you that you never leave or forsake me. I thank you for my miracle season and I speak life over the situations you have already promised me victory over. Thank you that your word is true, thank you for giving me life. Amen.

Your atmosphere must be guarded with the truth and those who truly believe. Who is supposed to be on this journey with you? Who is supposed to leave?

Day 14-Who Will You Have To Ignore?

1 Samuel 17:26-30 MSG

26 David, who was talking to the men standing around him, asked, "What's in it for the man who kills that Philistine and gets rid of this ugly blot on Israel's honor? Who does he think he is, anyway, this uncircumcised Philistine, taunting the armies of God-Alive?"27 They told him what everyone was saying about what the king would do for the man who killed the Philistine.28 Eliab, his older brother, heard David fraternizing with the men and lost his temper: "What are you doing here! Why aren't you minding your own business, tending that scrawny flock of sheep? I know what you're up to. You've come down here to see the sights, hoping for a ringside seat at a bloody battle!"29-30 "What is it with you?" replied David. "All I did was ask a question." Ignoring his brother, he turned to someone else, asked the same question, and got the same answer as before.

The timing of the Lord is important. The Lord told Samuel in the previous chapter that David would be King. This means the promise over David's life had already been announced in the earth so now it was time for the atmosphere to respond. Imagine dreaming, believing and waiting patiently for more (you've heard it, people tell you all the time you're destined for greatness, etc) but you haven't seen it yet. It was time for David to move because the Lord was with him. In the moment David could have let the voices of the naysayers stop or intimidate him into a delay. It was his moment and it was time for him to take it. Some people will forever see you as the person you were when they met you. Even inquiring into possibilities greater than what you've known can offend some people. Crazy right? Questions about wanting more can rub people the wrong way. I think it's the possibilities of you actually doing it that bothers them. I wonder if this was discouraging for David, after all, this was his older brother. Did he think before he responded? Or did he know at that moment that this was a part of his destiny? David had to ignore who they (family included) previously knew him to be and become who he was supposed to be.

Prayer:

Father, help me silence the voices of the naysayers, and walk into the fulfillment of the promise you have over my life. Help me to filter through the chatter to hear and follow your voice. Silence any voice that is not yours so that I may hear clearly. I need your guidance on what to prioritize in prayer and in my life. You have permission to be Lord over my actions and emotions. Amen.

You are strong enough to defeat any enemy that stands before you. What voices do you have to silence in order to do the will of the Lord?

Day 15-How Can I Follow When I Can't See?

1 Luke 1:34-38 NLT

34 Mary asked the angel, "But how can this happen? I am a virgin."35 The angel replied, "The Holy Spirit will come upon you, and the power of the Most High will overshadow you. So the baby to be born will be holy, and he will be called the Son of God. 36 What's more, your relative Elizabeth has become pregnant in her old age! People used to say she was barren, but she has conceived a son and is now in her sixth month. 37 For the word of God will never fail. 38 Mary responded, "I am the Lord's servant. May everything you have said about me come true." And then the angel left her.

The Lord was doing something new in the life of Mary. The journey she was about to embark upon would be one that had never been done before. She would be responsible for caring for a King, and not just any King but the King of Kings. One of the hardest things in faith to do, is to say yes when it makes no sense. Prior to this moment Mary was content with getting married to Joseph and living a common life. However, God had a better plan. Here comes the plot twist. So she was told something greater was coming but she didn't understand how. I am sure thoughts ran through her mind similar to the ones we have like, "this doesn't make sense, I don't have experience in that, or who will listen to me?". We get caught up in not being able to comprehend what he wants to take place and miss just getting in position. You will have to follow the voice of the Lord even when you cannot see. She didn't understand but in faith she made a decision to believe.

Prayer:

Lord I thank you for choosing me, I declare right now that I belong to you and that every promise you have released over my life has no choice but to manifest. I speak to that area of fear in my life and say go now, in the name of Jesus. You have no purpose here. Help me to be obedient and I thank you for the freedom to move in my purpose. I declare that I am the Lord's servant, Father may everything you have said about me come to true. Amen.

The Lord has planted something inside of all of us. There are blessings attached to your name. You are pregnant with a gift (idea or talent) that will bring forth an answer. What are you pregnant with? What has the Lord called you to deliver (produce)? What does the fruit of that look like?

Day 16-Watch What's Coming Out Of Your Mouth?

Proverbs 8:21 NLT

21 The tongue can bring death or life; those who love to talk will reap the consequences.

The Bible talks to us about the power of the tongue and the fruit that comes from it. We know that our words have power and what we release into the atmosphere will soon manifest. It is important to protect yourself from not only your words but from the words of others. Even simple things that we say like "I can't do this" or "it will never happen for me" are words that the enemy will use against us. Protect what you know to be true and destroy every lie. What is the truth you ask? The truth is what the Lord says about you and everything else is a lie. This also deals with vows we have made with ourselves, it's time to cut ties with heartbreak, disaster or whatever doesn't bring life to you. You can change the narrative, speak it and it will be so. You have the power "You will also decree a thing, and it will be established for you..." This also applies to things that we say about others, yes even the people you can't stand. Try speaking life over them, try praying for them (I know this may be hard) but you can do it. Watch how you distribute that power and what you empower.

Prayer:

Father help me guard my mouth and the things that come out of it. I ask that you would help me to be more account-able for the words that I release from my tongue. Sharpen my discernment that I would know what to say and in the season to say it. Amen.

It is important that you are slow to speak because it can save you. Has your mouth ever gotten you in trouble? What lessons have you learned from releasing words in love? and what lessons have you learned from releasing words in hate?

Day 17-What Does It Mean To Watch Over?

Jeremiah 1:12 AMPC

12 Then said the Lord to me, You have seen well, for I am alert and active, watching over My word to perform it.

The good news is, He always wins. As I was looking at that scripture it started to appear differently to me. The word "watching" stood out, so I had to look it up. One of the definitions for watch is to guard. When someone guards over something they protect it. He isn't just watching over His word He is protective over it to make sure it's performed. Oftentimes we think that the mistakes we have made are permanent. That they take us out of the running for the promise the Lord has for our life, but that is simply not true. He has NOT changed his mind about you, "He will perform His will". Allow the Holy Spirit to lead and guide you and He will always lead you back to Him. He is protective over you, rest in the assurance of that. The promise of the lord concerning your life MUST come to pass. The only thing above God is his word, declare his promises in faith! In return it creates a partnership with Him that you are also guarding His word. What does that look like?

It doesn't look like perfection but it does look like you are coming into alignment with the word of God.

Prayer:

Father, I bless your name for your grace and mercy. I thank you that I am not forgotten and the promises made over my life are just that: a Promise. I ask that you clear my vision so that I may see you and myself clearly. Thank you for watching over your word, help me to come in full alignment and partnership with the word concerning my life. I believe that You will perform Your will. Amen.

Your behavior will change, your outlook and ultimately the way you look at your situations.

What are the promises the Lord has made over your life? Who does the Lord say that you are?

Day 18-Why So Churchy?

Acts 11: 2-17 NIV

So when Peter went up to Jerusalem, the circumcised believers criticized him 3 and said, "You went into the house of uncircumcised men and ate with them." 4 Starting from the beginning, Peter told them the whole story: 5 "I was in the city of Joppa praying, and in a trance I saw a vision. I saw something like a large sheet being let down from heaven by its four corners, and it came down to where I was. 6 I looked into it and saw four-footed animals of the earth, wild beasts, reptiles and birds. 7 Then I heard a voice telling me, 'Get up, Peter. Kill and eat.' 8 "I replied, 'Surely not, Lord! Nothing impure or unclean has ever entered my mouth.' 9 "The voice spoke from heaven a second time, 'Do not call anything impure that God has made clean.' 10 This happened three times, and then it was all pulled up to heaven again. 11 "Right then three men who had been sent to me from Caesarea stopped at the house where I was staying. 12 The Spirit told me to have no hesitation about going with them. These six brothers also went with me, and we entered the man's house. 13 He told us how he had seen an angel appear in his house and say, 'Send to Joppa for Simon who is called Peter. 14 He will bring you a message through which you and all your household will be saved.' 15 "As I began to speak, the Holy

Spirit came on them as he had come on us at the beginning. 16 Then I remembered what the Lord had said: 'John baptized with[a] water, but you will be baptized with the Holy Spirit.' 17 So if God gave them the same gift he gave us who believed in the Lord Jesus Christ, who was I to think that I could stand in God's way?"

Just as the Lord brings revelation to us in different ways he also brings this revelation to all of his people. The Lord is moving us away from a separated church and a separated understanding of who He is. His word says that He would give us a heart to know him. We should have a kingdom mindset, that means the church is one body and that one body includes all denominations. I may not worship exactly like you , preach exactly like you or sing the same songs as you do. But in the sight of God we are all his servants. One of the most powerful settings for the Holy Spirit to move in, is an atmosphere full of believers of all races and all nationalities together worshiping as one. The Lord is no respecter of persons and if he isn't then why should We. I used to read this scripture and would shake my head, like Peter thinks so much of himself. Funny, I never thought about my own issues of pride. If you know me, then you know I describe being saved in two phases - being saved (worldly way everybody loves Jesus) and being saved for real, for real (living for Christ) How easy it is for us to think so highly of ourselves and our relationship with God that we can't receive from anybody else.

Prayer:
Father, help me to not be judgmental, I ask for forgiveness for not seeing others the way that you see them. I ask that help bring your people together on one accord through your word and your truth. Deal with our heart posture so that we may understand the heart of you. Amen.

Search the scripture and your heart to see what you have deemed unworthy that the Lord has cleansed. In what ways have you been religious? How can I see others the way that the Lord sees them?

Day 19-What's Your Testimony?

Revelations 12:11 KJV

11 And they overcame him by the blood of the Lamb, and by the word of their testimony; and they loved not their lives unto the death

The blood of Christ can defeat ANYTHING! You have weapons, it is time to use them. Now, I know that you have heard about the blood, but have you heard what your testimony can do? Our voice gives way to light and helps other believers know they are not alone. It encourages us to remember and reflect on what he has already done. Honestly it is hard for me to stay in the sunken place hearing the testimony of God. Not just in the lives of others but in my own life, if he did it before, he can do it again". Rejoice I say, rejoice for the victory of the Lord belongs to you and from that place you are unstoppable. He has given us the power to deliver and set the captives free. Don't be afraid to share (with discernment) with others what he has delivered you from. Allow the Lord to not only work in you but through you and into the lives of others.

Prayer:

Father, I thank you for my voice, I thank you for remembering me, I thank you that what the enemy meant for bad you are going to use it for good. Help me to be a voice in the wilderness for your people, help me to use my story to free others. Amen.

"We will overcome by the blood of the lamb and the word of our testimony", and It's time to free others. What keeps you from sharing your testimony? What is the last thing the Lord has done for you? What testimony have you heard that has helped free you?

Day 20-Can You Honor The Dis-Honorable?

Samuel 24:1-8 NIV

24 After Saul returned from pursuing the Philistines, he was told, "David is in the Desert of En Gedi." 2 So Saul took three thousand able young men from all Israel and set out to look for David and his men near the Crags of the Wild Goats. 3 He came to the sheep pens along the way; a cave was there, and Saul went in to relieve himself. David and his men were far back in the cave. 4 The men said, "This is the day the Lord spoke of when he said to you, 'I will give your enemy into your hands for you to deal with as you wish.'" Then David crept up unnoticed and cut off a corner of Saul's robe. 5 Afterward, David was conscience-stricken for having cut off a corner of his robe. 6 He said to his men, "The Lord forbid that I should do such a thing to my master, the Lord's anointed, or lay my hand on him; for he is the anointed of the Lord." 7 With these words David sharply rebuked his men and did not allow them to attack Saul. And Saul left the cave and went his way. 8 Then David went out of the cave and called out to Saul, "My lord the king!" When Saul looked behind him, David bowed down and prostrated himself with his face to the ground.

On this journey with Christ, a major thing I had to learn to get over was loving people who I knew didn't mean me well. This is something I continuously have to work at. As frustrated as it may make me feel, I have to submit all of it to the feet of Jesus. I don't know why early in my career it was such a shock for me to witness people's actions or behavior be so different from who they said they were. I was so annoyed like "Lord, do you see what they are doing, now you know they're not right", "what are you going to do about it" or "Why do they get away with doing whatever, but I can't do nothing". Sounds like the words of a mature adult, huh? I believe I was so irritated because it felt like they were winning and I was losing, stuck being their help. The Lord commands us to be more like Christ, not more like "them". The Lord is teaching us to honor the dishonorable. I had to move past what I saw and see what He saw. The Lord has to know that he could trust us to submit to His will over our own. David could have easily taken Saul out but he chose to stop and consult God to see what He wanted to do. We must honor the anointing in our life even when we see the flaws in their character.

Prayer:

Father help me move past my emotions and feelings and into the insight of the Holy Spirit. I ask that you forgive me for taking matters into my own hands and judging others. Help me to have a servant's heart toward the people you have placed over me. Help me to honor the people that you have put in my life and the anointing you have placed on them. I ask that you forgive me for letting my emotions rule how I love. Amen.

Just because you have the power to punish or harm someone doesn't mean you should do it.

What is the Lord saying to you about your current leadership? How have you submitted to their authority or vision? What are the areas you need to work on?

Day 21-How Are You Living?

1 Peter 2:9-12 NLT

9 But you are not like that, for you are a chosen people. You are royal priests,[a] a holy nation, God's very own possession. As a result, you can show others the goodness of God, for he called you out of the darkness into his wonderful light. 10 "Once you had no identity as a people; now you are God's people. Once you received no mercy; now you have received God's mercy." 11 Dear friends, I warn you as "temporary residents and foreigners" to keep away from worldly desires that wage war against your very souls. 12 Be careful to live properly among your unbelieving neighbors. Then even if they accuse you of doing wrong, they will see your honorable behavior, and they will give honor to God when he judges the world.

Crazy thing is that before I knew I was special, other people noticed it. However, because it wasn't something I saw, I didn't understand it. Once I came into agreement with who I was in Christ and how he viewed me, the way that I viewed my life started to change. I grew up in church and gave my life to Christ at an early age. However I was so young and hadn't really experienced anything so I didn't really understand the reason behind living for Christ. Once I had lived a little I got saved " for real for real". I'm sure you're wondering what "saved real for real" means. Well this represents for me when I decided to change my lifestyle and desired to live holy. I wanted to be more than just a reader of the word but become a doer. This brought on an understanding of what it means to live Holy. I started to identify as a daughter who was special, Queen Ester. It is not easy which is why the bible warns us of it, "keep away from worldly desires that wage war against your soul". This would determine the places and the things I got to experience in God. If I was going to win souls to Christ my behavior would have to be a reflection of that. People are watching to see if this is all really real. They are curious about you and your God.

Prayer:
Father, I thank you that my identity is found in you. I thank you that you chose me and that you have mercy on me. Help me to honor you through my actions. Help me to stay away from worldly desires that would wage war against my soul. All of me belongs to you and I am thankful for that covenant. Amen.

Let them find your behavior honorable. What will they witness from you? What are the things currently in your life that are after your soul? What do you consider honorable behavior?

Day 22-Do You Really Believe?

Mark 9:24, 28-29 NKJV

24 Immediately the father of the child cried out and said with tears, "Lord, I believe; help my unbelief!" 28 And when He had come into the house, His disciples asked Him privately, "Why could we not cast it out?" 29 So He said to them, "This kind can come out by nothing but prayer and fasting."

As I begin to mature in Christ I would have people around me encouraging me. Saying things like, " You know, you're special" and " the Lord is going to heal you" and I thought I believed them. However, once I started to deal with disappointment and long suffering , I wondered when it would actually happen for me. Sure he could do it, but it didn't seem like he was doing it for me. My faith was really being tested, did I believe for others and not myself? I had to arrive at a place where I was honest with the Lord about what I was dealing with. I had to trust him, with my truth which was that I was struggling to believe what He had said about me. I was embarrassed to admit that but so much break through (deliverance) came in my situation once I was honest and gave the Father all of me, even the parts struggling to believe. This is when fasting and prayer took center stage. Jesus told the disciples that " this kind can only come out by prayer and fasting". There will be things that challenge what you believe but I dare you to put the word on it and see what he does with your sacrifice. Through this He exposed the areas of my life that left the door open to the enemy. I got strategy and clarity about how he wanted to defeat the giants in my life at the time. You are not doing this alone, ask the father for help.

Prayer:

Father I come to you knowing that when I am weak, that is when you are made strong. relinquish control and all of my emotions to you. Help me overcome doubt and fear. Show me where the areas of my unbelief are rooted and make me whole in you. I walk in total faith believing what you have said about me. I trust you to handle all parts of me. Amen.

Seeing this scripture in the bible let us know that it is not uncommon for believers to feel this way. What do you struggle believing that the Lord has told you about yourself? What are your areas of unbelief? Are you honest with the Lord about how you feel? What do you need to fast and pray about?

Day 23-Are You Confident In Who He Has Called You To Be?

Exodus 4:10-17 NIV

10 Moses said to the Lord, "Pardon your servant, Lord. I have never been eloquent, neither in the past nor since you have spoken to your servant. I am slow of speech and tongue." 11 The Lord said to him, "Who gave human beings their mouths? Who makes them deaf or mute? Who gives them sight or makes them blind? Is it not I, the Lord? 12 Now go; I will help you speak and will teach you what to say." 13 But Moses said, "Pardon your servant, Lord. Please send someone else." 14 Then the Lord's anger burned against Moses and he said, "What about your brother, Aaron the Levite? I know he can speak well. He is already on his way to meet you, and he will be glad to see you. 15 You shall speak to him and put words in his mouth; I will help both of you speak and will teach you what to do. 16 He will speak to the people for you, and it will be as if he were your mouth and as if you were God to him. 17 But take this staff in your hand so you can perform the signs with it."

It is time for you to speak to witness and help bring others out. We don't always feel comfortable to do what the Lord has called us to do. I mean look at Moses, sure we know him as this powerful leader who saw the face of God but in the beginning he was timid, scared and had a stuttering problem. He felt like the only way to accomplish what the Lord said was to get someone to do it with him. I wonder if Aaron was what the Lord initially had in mind or if Moses had just given a simple yes could he have done this alone? When I was younger, if my mom told me to go somewhere or do something I would ask if a friend could come with me. In my mind my insecurities diminished when I had someone with me, the funny part is, I already had someone with me, God.

Prayer:

Father, I thank you for how you have created me. I bless you for the plans and the promises that you have over my life. Help me to be confident in who you have called me to be. Help me to not see with my physical eyes but with the spiritual eyes of the Lord. Lord replace any doubt and fear that I may have with confidence and love from you. I submit myself to your will. Amen.

Fear not sister for He is with you and be confident in who he has called you to be. What are your insecurities? How has that served as a hindrance in the past? What has it blocked you from doing? What are you being sent out to do?

Day 24-What Do You See, Beauty Or Ashes?

Isaiah 61:3 NIV

3 and provide for those who grieve in Zion—to bestow on them a crown of beauty instead of ashes, the oil of joy instead of mourning, and a garment of praise instead of a spirit of despair. They will be called oaks of righteousness, a planting of the Lord for the display of his splendor.

I think it's important for any believer to know that the Lord is a keeper of his word and he makes all things new. Not only is he a keeper but gives beauty for ashes. What that means is the things that you have gone through that makes you feel ugly unworthy or used. He provides beauty for all of that. He replaces those stains with beauty, you will not look like what you have been through. A refinement process has taken place, partner with the Father on this. Allow the fire of god to create something new in you.

Prayer:
Father I thank you, that you make everything good. I thank you for your restoration power and your love. Help me to

willingly give you all the things that I am afraid of, ashamed of or have hurt me in the past to you. I thank you for the great exchange, that you are giving me beauty for ashes. That you call me righteous and beautiful. Thank you for reminding me of what I am. Help me to see myself the way that you see me. Amen.

You don't have to weep anymore over the things that once had you down. The Lord has already made an exchange with you, beauty for ashes. It is time to dance, this is your season.

Day 25-What Is The Lord's Decree Over Your Life?

Amos 9:13-15 msg

*13-15 "Yes indeed, it won't be long now." God's Decree.
"Things are going to happen so fast your head will swim, one thing fast on the heels of the other. You won't be able to keep up. Everything will be happening at once—and everywhere you look, blessings! Blessings like wine pouring off the mountains and hills. I'll make everything right again for my people Israel: "They'll rebuild their ruined cities. They'll plant vineyards and drink good wine. They'll work their gardens and eat fresh vegetables. And I'll plant them, plant them on their own land. They'll never again be uprooted from the land I've given them." God, your God, says so.*

The last day of this devotional should be blessings declared over you. This is my go to scripture whenever I am in need of a little encouragement. Let this serve as a reminder of what the Lord is going to do. The things you have lost will be restored and blessings are all around you. Whenever I read this scripture, I get a visual. I can literally see the wine pouring off the mountain tops. There is nothing higher than God except

His word and He has promised to make everything right again. As you end this devotional review the list you made in the beginning of what you are believing God for (healing, breakthrough, restoration of relationships, manifestation, etc.). Take inventory of what he has already started to rebuild and write down what He is speaking to you.

Prayer:

Father I declare, complete restoration and healing to the person reading this. I pray that you answer them speedily according to your will, bringing forth revelation and understanding. I pray that whatever they ask according to your will, shall be done. I pray that they believe again. This is their overflow season, overwhelm them with Your love. Amen.

What is the Lord declaring over you? Write out what He is speaking to you and create a prayer based on what you hear.

 Brittany is a native of Georgia. She obtained her bachelor's degree from Tuskegee University and MBA from the University of Georgia. Brittany is a passionate leader and teacher, dedicated to empowering, shaping and healing women; helping to lead them into their purpose. She is trained in deliverance, operates in ministry leadership, and loves to serve. Her sweet and spicy personality helps move women from religion and into the real. Her mission is to heal the broken and break cycles allowing individuals to reach their full potential.